JULY 13, 2009. SONIA MARIA SOTOMAYOR RAISES HER RIGHT HAND TO BE SWORN IN BEFORE THE U.S. SENATE JUDICIARY COMMITTEE.

SHE WILL ENDURE FOUR GRUELING DAYS OF HEARINGS.

WHEN THE SMOKE CLEARS, SHE WILL HAVE WON CONFIRMATION TO THE LIFETIME APPOINTMENT BY A 68-31 MARGIN. IN THE SPACE OF A FEW WEEKS, SHE WILL HAVE BECOME ONE OF THE MOST POWERFUL WOMEN IN AMERICA.

AND WHEN THE COURT RECONVENE IN SEPTEMBER, SHE WILL SLIP ON HER BLACK ROBES TAKE HER PLACE ALONG SIDE THE OTHER MEMBERS OF AMERICA'S MOST AUGUST JUDICIAL BODY.

BUT AFTER ALL THAT SCRUTINY, HOW WELL WILL WE REALLY KNOW HER? CAN WE TRUST HER TO RULE JUSTLY AND FAIRLY ON THE CONSTITUTIONAL ISSUES THAT AFFECT ALL OUR LIVES?

JUST WHO IS THIS WOMAN AND HOW DID SHE COME TO BE INVESTED WITH SUCH POWER?

JUSTICE SOTOMAYOR'S STORY BEGINS, AS ALL GREAT STORIES DO, IN A PUBLIC HOSPITAL IN THE BRONX, ON JUNE 25, 1954. IT WAS A VERY HOT AND HUMID DAY. TRUST ME. I LOOKED IT UP.

MATERNITY

SONIA'S FIRST HOME WAS A TINY TENEMENT IN THE SOUTH BRONX. HER FATHER, JUAN, A NATIVE OF PUERTO RICO, WAS A TOOL-AND-DIE WORKER WITH A THIRD-GRADE EDUCATION. WHILE HE SPOKE NO ENGLISH, HE WAS FLUENT IN THE LANGUAGE OF HARD WORK.

EMPIRE Tool & DIE

HER MOTHER, CELINA BÁEZ, WORKED AS A TELEPHONE OPERATOR. SHE LATER BECAME A LICENSED PRACTICAL NURSE.

SONIA'S YOUNGER BROTHER JUAN COMPLETED THE FAMILY PORTRAIT IN 1957.

THAT SAME YEAR, THE FAMILY LEFT THEIR CRAMPED TENEMENT FOR COMPARATIVELY SPACIOUS LODGINGS AT THE BRONXDALE HOUSES HOUSING PROJECT. THE NEW DIGS WERE CLEANER, SAFER, AND MORE RACIALLY AND ETHNICALLY DIVERSE.

ALL THINGS CONSIDERED, IT WASN'T SUCH A BAD LIFE. THE CATHOLIC CHURCH SUPPLIED ORDER, RITUAL, AND A SET OF RULES TO LIVE BY.

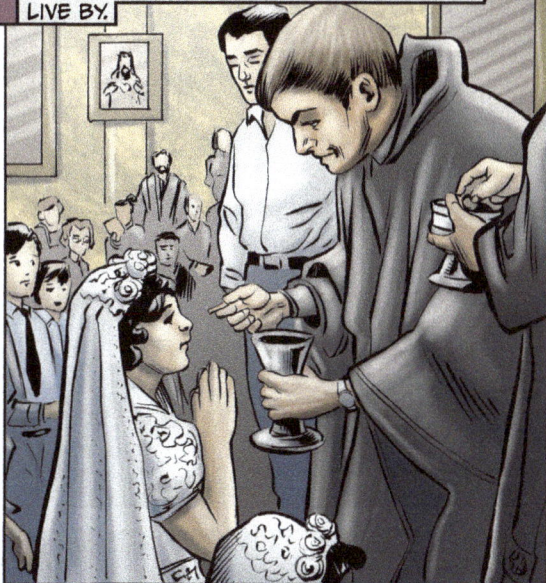

LIVING IN THE BRONX, SHE NATURALLY BECAME A FAN OF THE NEIGHBORHOOD BASEBALL TEAM, A RAGTAG LITTLE OUTFIT KNOWN AS THE NEW YORK YANKEES.

FOR ENTERTAINMENT, SONIA WENT TO THE MOVIES REGULARLY. ONE OF HER FAVORITE PERFORMERS WAS CANTINFLAS, THE MEXICAN FILM COMEDIAN WHO HAS BEEN CALLED "MEXICO'S ANSWER TO JERRY LEWIS."

AND IN THE SUMMERS, THE FAMILY HEADED OFF TO PUERTO RICO FOR A LITTLE FUN IN THE SUN.

LIFE WASN'T ALL POTATO PANCAKES AND APPLESAUCE OF COURSE. WHEN SHE WAS EIGHT YEARS OLD, SONIA WAS DIAGNOSED WITH JUVENILE DIABETES. SHE STARTED TAKING DAILY INSULIN INJECTIONS.

WHEN SHE WAS NINE, SONIA'S FATHER DIED. IF HAVING TO CHECK HER BLOOD SUGAR THREE TIMES A DAY DIDN'T INSTILL SELF-DISCIPLINE AND INDEPENDENCE, BEING THE OLDEST CHILD OF A SINGLE MOTHER SURE DID.

LUCKILY SONIA WAS AN AVID READER AND COULD FIND TEMPORARY RESPITE FROM HER TROUBLES IN THE ADVENTURES OF THAT PLUCKY "GIRL DETECTIVE," NANCY DREW.

AND OF COURSE THERE WAS ALWAYS TELEVISION—PERRY MASON, TO BE EXACT. IN THE ABSENCE OF HER DAD, RAYMOND BURR'S UNFLAPPABLE TV LAWYER BECAME SONIA'S PRINCIPAL ROLE MODEL.

"I WAS GOING TO COLLEGE AND I WAS GOING TO BECOME AN ATTORNEY," SHE SAID. "I KNEW THAT WHEN I WAS TEN."

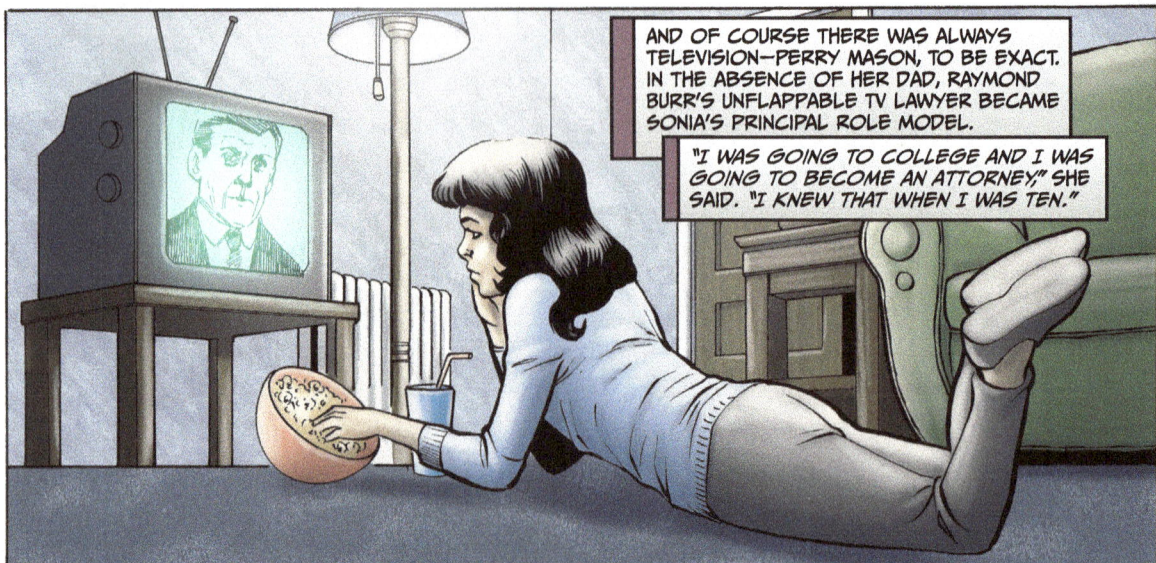

ONCE SHE HAD SET HER GOAL, THERE WAS NO STOPPING HER. EVEN MORE IMPORTANTLY, SHE HAD HER MOTHER IN HER CORNER. CELINA SOTOMAYOR MADE A POINT OF BUYING THE FAMILY A COMPLETE SET OF THE ENCYCLOPEDIA BRITANNICA.

ALL THAT SELF-DIRECTED READING PAID OFF. AT THE BLESSED SACRAMENT SCHOOL, SONIA WAS CLASS VALEDICTORIAN AND COMPILED A NEAR-PERFECT ATTENDANCE RECORD.

WHEN SHE WASN'T READING OR STUDYING, SONIA WAS WORKING—IN A LOCAL STORE, AT FIRST, AND LATER AT A HOSPITAL.

ABOUT THE ONLY THING STANDING IN THE WAY OF HIGH ACHIEVEMENT WERE HER SURROUNDINGS. OF LATE, THE ONCE-PRISTINE BRONXDALE HOUSES HAD BECOME A GODFORSAKEN HELLHOLE—RIFE WITH GANGS, JUNKIES, AND PETTY CRIME.

SO IN 1970, WHEN SONIA WAS 16, THE FAMILY PICKED UP AND LEFT, MOVING TO THE CO-OP CITY RESIDENTIAL APARTMENT COMPLEX IN A SAFER, MORE PROSPEROUS PART OF THE BRONX.

SONIA NOW COMMUTED EVERY MORNING TO THE ACADEMICALLY RIGOROUS CARDINAL SPELLMAN HIGH SCHOOL.

CSI: Sotomayor

VOTE SONIA!

THERE SHE JOINED THE SCHOOL FORENSICS TEAM...

...SERVED IN STUDENT GOVERNMENT AND GRADUATED—YEP, YOU GUESSED IT—VALEDICTORIAN OF HER SENIOR CLASS.

IN THE FALL OF 1972, SONIA MOVED ON TO COLLEGE AT PRINCETON UNIVERSITY.

MORNING, CHIP! HOW'D YOUR SQUASH GAME WITH MUFFY GO?

CORKING, CHAD! SIMPLY CORKING!

THERE WAS A DIFFICULT PERIOD OF ADJUSTMENT FOR THIS DAUGHTER OF THE BRONX, ATTENDING ONE OF THE MOST ELITE—AND LILY WHITE—OF ALL IVY LEAGUE SCHOOLS. AT FIRST, SONIA LATER SAID, SHE FELT LIKE "A VISITOR LANDING IN AN ALIEN COUNTRY." CALL IT "PLANET PREP."

HA HA HA HA HA! RIPPING! VERY WITTY!

AND SO I SAID TO HENRY L. STIMSON, "MR. SECRETARY, IF YOU RUN THIS COUNTRY'S FOREIGN POLICY ANYTHING LIKE YOU STEER THIS YACHT...

...WE SHALL ALL BE VOTING FOR ROOSEVELT IN THE NEXT ELECTION!"

FOR HER ENTIRE FRESHMAN YEAR, SHE WAS TOO INTIMIDATED TO SPEAK UP IN CLASS.

IN TIME, SONIA WAS ABLE TO OVERCOME HER CLASS ANXIETY.

DETERMINED TO IMPROVE HER LANGUAGE SKILLS, SHE PUT IN LONG HOURS AT THE LIBRARY STUDYING THE CLASSICS.

CICERO

HOMER
Shakespeare
The Odyssey

BY GEORGE, YOU'VE GOT IT!

SHE WORKED WITH A PROFESSOR OUTSIDE OF CLASS TO INCREASE HER KNOWLEDGE BASE AND IMPROVE HER POISE AND CONFIDENCE.

AND SHE NEVER LOST TOUCH WITH HER HERITAGE. SHE DEVOTED HER SENIOR THESIS TO THE TOPIC OF PUERTO RICO'S STRUGGLE FOR INDEPENDENCE UNDER THE LEADERSHIP OF LUIS MUÑOZ MARÍN.

TIME

SHE BECAME ACTIVE IN CAMPUS POLITICS, RALLYING PRINCETON'S LATINO COMMUNITY ON BEHALF OF PUERTO RICAN STUDENT RECRUITMENT AND FACULTY HIRING.

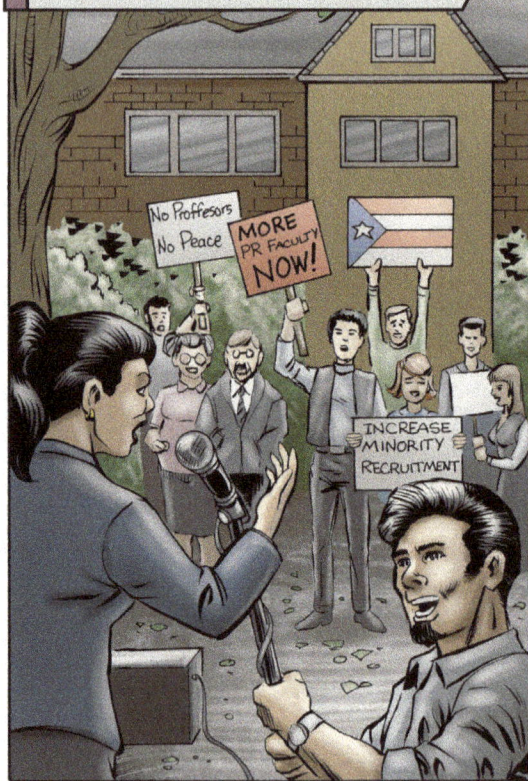

No Proffesors No Peace

MORE PR FACULTY NOW!

INCREASE MINORITY RECRUITMENT

OFF-CAMPUS, SHE SPENT HER TIME VOLUNTEERING WITH LATINO PATIENTS AT THE TRENTON PSYCHIATRIC HOSPITAL.

IT WAS THE HARDEST FOUR YEARS OF HER LIFE THUS FAR, BUT SONIA GRADUATED SUMMA CUM LAUDE IN 1976. AN IVY LEAGUE DEGREE WAS HERS AT LAST.

SHAKE SHAKE SHAKE... SHAKE SHAKE SHAKE... SHAKE YOUR BOOTY!

BUT GRADUATING FROM COLLEGE WASN'T SONIA'S ONLY REASON FOR CELEBRATING. THAT SUMMER, SHE MARRIED LONGTIME BOYFRIEND KEVIN EDWARD NOONAN. SHE NOW STYLED HERSELF SONIA SOTOMAYOR DE NOONAN.

AND WHEN THE PARTY ENDED, SHE GOT RIGHT BACK TO BUSINESS. SHE ENROLLED IN YALE LAW SCHOOL, WHERE SHE BECAME AN EDITOR ON THE PRESTIGIOUS LAW JOURNAL.

AFTER SECURING HER LAW DEGREE IN 1979, SONIA WAS QUICKLY SCOOPED UP BY FAMED MANHATTAN DISTRICT ATTORNEY ROBERT MORGENTHAU, WHO HAD A REPUTATION FOR HIRING ONLY THE BEST, MOST QUALIFIED LAWYERS IN THE COUNTRY.

IT WAS THE BEST TRAINING GROUND A YOUNG LAWYER COULD ASK FOR. UNDER MORGENTHAU'S GUIDANCE, SONIA PROSECUTED EVERYTHING FROM SHOPLIFTING AND PROSTITUTION CASES TO MURDERS, ASSAULTS, AND ROBBERIES.

IN HER HIGHEST PROFILE CASE, SONIA HELPED CONVICT THE SO-CALLED "TARZAN MURDERER"— A LUNATIC WHO KILLED PEOPLE AFTER SWINGING INTO THEIR APARTMENT WINDOWS.

MORGENTHAU EFFUSIVELY SANG HER PRAISES, CALLING HER A "FEARLESS AND EFFECTIVE PROSECUTOR."

AFTER A WHILE, HOWEVER, THE HIGH-PRESSURE JOB TOOK ITS TOLL. BURNED OUT, SHE LEFT THE D.A.'S OFFICE IN 1983. "AFTER A WHILE, YOU FORGET THERE ARE DECENT, LAW-ABIDING PEOPLE IN LIFE," SONIA SAID LATER.

ANOTHER CASUALTY OF THE JOB WAS HER MARRIAGE TO KEVIN EDWARD NOONAN. THEY DIVORCED THAT SAME YEAR.

FLUSSSHHHH!

IN 1984, SONIA WENT INTO PRIVATE PRACTICE WITH A CORPORATE LAW FIRM.

HERE'S YOUR PAYCHECK, SONIA. WELCOME TO THE FIRM!

GA-GA-GA-GOING!!!

ATTORN
SONIA
SOTOMA

IT WAS A CHANCE FOR HER TO TRY AND ARGUE MORE CASES IN COURT—AND TO MAKE SOME REAL CHEDDAR FOR THE FIRST TIME IN HER LIFE.

RETAIL

Su

CLOSED
NEW YORK CITY
JUDICIAL DEPT.

MANY OF HER CLIENTS WERE INTERNATIONAL CORPORATIONS DOING BUSINESS IN THE UNITED STATES. SHE SPENT MOST OF HER TIME TRACKING DOWN AND SUING PEOPLE WHO SOLD COUNTERFEIT LUXURY HANDBAGS.

AFTER ONE SUCH CASE, SONIA TOOK PART IN A RITUAL CRUSHING BY GARBAGE TRUCK OF 9000 ERSATZ FENDI HANDBAGS STAGED AT NEW YORK CITY'S TAVERN ON THE GREEN RESTAURANT.

AFTER TWO YEARS OF CHASING HANDBAG BANDITS, HOWEVER, SONIA ONCE AGAIN GREW BORED WITH HER JOB.

IN 1986, SHE APPEARED ON THE ABC MORNING SHOW GOOD MORNING AMERICA, WHERE SHE COMPLAINED THAT THE VAST MAJORITY OF THE WORK SHE HAD DONE SINCE LAW SCHOOL WAS PURE DRUDGERY.

IT WAS TIME FOR ANOTHER CAREER CHANGE. IN 1988, SHE ACCEPTED AN OFFER FROM NEW YORK CITY MAYOR ED KOCH TO SERVE ON THE CITY'S NEWLY FORMED CAMPAIGN FINANCE BOARD. SHE REMAINED IN THAT JOB FOR THE NEXT FOUR YEARS.

HOW'M I DOIN'?

IF I AM RE-ELECTED, I WILL MAKE SURE WE GET A LATINO JUDGE ON THE U.S. DISTRICT COURT..

MOYNIHAN ☆ FOR ☆ SENATE

MOYNIHAN '88

MEANWHILE, NEW YORK'S SENIOR U.S. SENATOR, DANIEL PATRICK MOYNIHAN, WAS SEARCHING AROUND FOR A QUALIFIED HISPANIC TO ELEVATE TO THE POSITION OF DISTRICT COURT JUDGE.

AFTER HIS RE-ELECTION, A MEMBER OF MOYNIHAN'S STAFF CAME TO HIM WITH THE FOLLOWING RECOMMENDATION.

HAVE WE GOT A JUDGE FOR YOU!

WITH THE HELP OF HIS GOP COUNTERPART, ALPHONSE D'AMATO (WHO HAD AGREED TO SIGN OFF ON ALL JUDICIAL RECOMMENDATIONS), MOYNIHAN GOT SONIA APPOINTED TO THE BENCH BY REPUBLICAN PRESIDENT GEORGE H.W. BUSH.

GREAT CHOICE, FELLAS! NOW...WHO'S FOR PORK RINDS?

WITH ONE STROKE OF A PEN, SONIA SOTOMAYOR BECAME THE YOUNGEST JUDGE IN THE SOUTHERN DISTRICT, THE FIRST HISPANIC FEDERAL JUDGE IN NEW YORK STATE, AND THE FIRST PUERTO RICAN WOMAN TO SERVE AS A JUDGE ON A U.S. FEDERAL COURT.

SHE DEVELOPED A REPUTATION AS A TOUGH-AS-NAILS, PRO-PROSECUTION JUDGE KNOWN FOR DOLING OUT STIFF SENTENCES.

HANG 'IM HIGH, BOYS! HANG 'IM HIGH!

CIVIL CASES CAME BEFORE HER AS WELL. IN 1995, SHE ISSUED THE INJUNCTION THAT ENDED THE 232-DAY LONG MAJOR LEAGUE BASEBALL STRIKE.

IT'S GREAT TO BE "PLAYING BALL" ONCE AGAIN, EH, JUDGE SOTOMAYOR?

YOU GOT THAT RIGHT, COMMISSIONER ALLAN "BUD" SELIG!

THAT SAME YEAR, SHE RULED AGAINST THE AUTHOR OF A BOOK OF *SEINFELD* TV TRIVIA, CITING INFRINGEMENT OF COPYRIGHT AGAINST THE SHOW'S CREATORS.

SHE EVEN DEFIED THE WHITE HOUSE WHEN SHE ISSUED A RULING ALLOWING THE *WALL STREET JOURNAL* TO PUBLISH THE SUICIDE NOTE OF FORMER DEPUTY WHITE HOUSE COUNSEL VINCE FOSTER.

Vince Foster

IN 1997, FOSTER'S FORMER BOSS, PRESIDENT BILL CLINTON, REWARDED SONIA FOR HER EVEN-HANDED JUDGMENT BY NOMINATING HER TO THE U.S. COURT OF APPEALS FOR THE SECOND CIRCUIT.

CONGRATULATIONS, JUDGE! HAVE A CIGAR?

OVER THE NEXT DECADE, SHE WOULD HEAR APPEALS IN MORE THAN 3,000 CASES AND WRITE MORE THAN 380 OPINIONS.

SHE GAINED A REPUTATION FOR RUNNING A "HOT BENCH"— LEGALSPEAK FOR ASKING TOUGH, SOMETIMES BELLIGERENT QUESTIONS OF LAWYERS WHO ARGUED CASES BEFORE HER.

SHE ALSO FOUND HERSELF IN HIGH DEMAND ON THE PUBLIC SPEAKING CIRCUIT. SHE APPEARED FREQUENTLY BEFORE GROUPS OF HISPANIC LAW SCHOOL STUDENTS.

EVERY NIGHT SHE RETURNED TO THE TASTEFULLY DECORATED HOME SHE HAD PURCHASED IN NEW YORK CITY'S GREENWICH VILLAGE. SHE LIVED MODESTLY, FOR SOMEONE OF SUCH IMMENSE POWER AND INFLUENCE.

SHE STILL HAD TO GIVE HERSELF DAILY INSULIN INJECTIONS, A REGULAR REMINDER THAT DIABETES CAN BE CONTROLLED, BUT NEVER CURED.

AS FOR ROMANCE...AS THEY SAY IN NEW YORK: FUGGEDABOUTIT. HER WORK ON THE COURT OF APPEALS CONSUMED NEARLY ALL OF HER TIME. "I HAVE FOUND IT DIFFICULT TO MAINTAIN A RELATIONSHIP WHILE I'VE PURSUED MY CAREER," SHE ADMITTED.

SHE WAS BRIEFLY ENGAGED TO A NEW YORK CONSTRUCTION MAGNATE, PETER WHITE, BUT THEIR RELATIONSHIP ENDED IN 2000, BEFORE THEY TIED THE KNOT. SONIA WAS REDUCED TO EATING TAKEOUT FOOD AND BURYING HERSELF IN HER WORK ONCE MORE.

JUST ABOUT THE MOST THRILLING THING THAT HAPPENED TO HER IN THIS PERIOD OCCURRED IN NOVEMBER OF 2008, WHEN SHE WON $8,283 PLAYING THE SLOTS AT A LOCAL CASINO.

GENERAL TSO'S CHICKEN! THIS ISN'T WHAT I ORDERED! WHERE'S MY MOO GOO GAI PAN?

AWWWW YYYEAAAHH!

JUDGE SONIA NEEDS A NEW SET OF ROBES!

LUCKY FOR SONIA, SOMEONE ELSE HIT THE JACKPOT THAT MONTH AS WELL. BARACK HUSSEIN OBAMA WAS ELECTED PRESIDENT OF THE UNITED STATES.

SONIA MAY NOT HAVE KNOWN IT YET, BUT THE GRAY, LONELY LIFE OF AN OBSCURE APPELLATE JUDGE WAS ABOUT TO COME TO AN END FOR HER...FOR GOOD!

ON MAY 26, 2009, PRESIDENT OBAMA NOMINATED SONIA TO REPLACE THE RETIRING JUSTICE DAVID SOUTER ON THE U.S. SUPREME COURT. SHE WOULD BE ONLY THE THIRD WOMAN AND THE FIRST HISPANIC TO SERVE ON THE HIGH COURT.

SONIA, WHAT YOU'VE SHOWN IN YOUR LIFE IS THAT IT DOESN'T MATTER WHERE YOU COME FROM, WHAT YOU LOOK LIKE, OR WHAT CHALLENGES LIFE THROWS YOUR WAY -- NO DREAM IS BEYOND REACH IN THE UNITED STATES OF AMERICA!

ALMOST IMMEDIATELY, THE MEDIA AND CONSERVATIVE CRITICS SEIZED ON COMMENTS SONIA HAD MADE DURING AN ADDRESS TO HISPANIC LAW STUDENTS AT THE UNIVERSITY OF CALIFORNIA AT BERKELEY SEVERAL YEARS BEFORE.

I WOULD HOPE THAT A WISE LATINA WOMAN WITH THE RICHNESS OF HER EXPERIENCES WOULD MORE OFTEN THAN NOT REACH A BETTER CONCLUSION THAN A WHITE MALE WHO HASN'T LIVED THAT LIFE.

AND THERE WAS A WHOLE SEPARATE KERFUFFLE OVER A RULING SHE HAD ISSUED IN A DISCRIMINATION CASE INVOLVING A GROUP OF DISGRUNTLED WHITE NEW HAVEN FIREFIGHTERS.

WITHIN DAYS, SONIA WAS BEING DENOUNCED AS A RACIST.

ONE RIGHT-WING FORMER CONGRESSMAN EVEN ATTACKED HER MEMBERSHIP IN THE MAINSTREAM HISPANIC CIVIL RIGHTS ORGANIZATION, LA RAZA.

LA RAZA IS NOTHING MORE THAN A LATINO KKK WITHOUT THE HOODS OR THE NOOSES!

msnbc

RUSH LIMBAUGH ATTACKED HER ON THE RADIO...

OBAMA IS THE GREATEST LIVING EXAMPLE OF A REVERSE RACIST AND NOW HE'S APPOINTED ONE TO THE SUPREME COURT!

NEWT GINGRICH SAVAGED HER ON TWITTER.

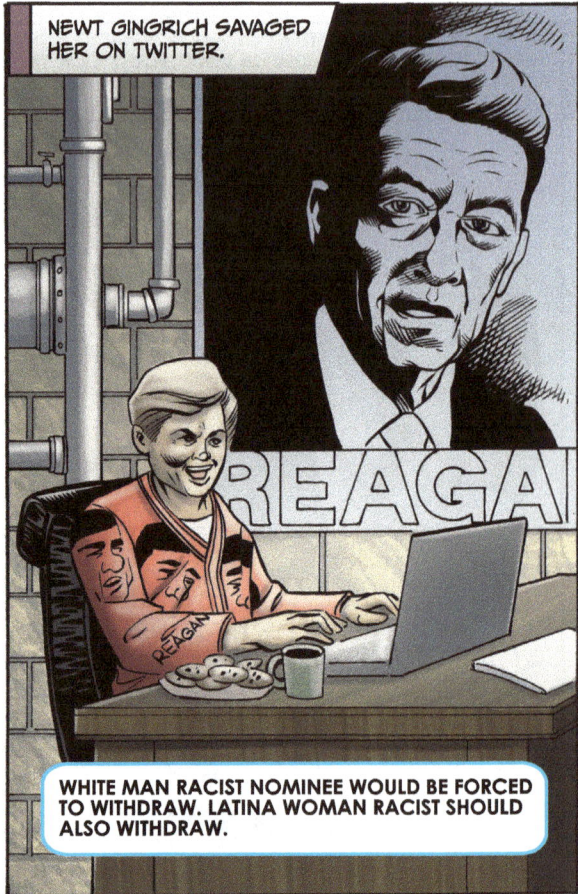

REAGA[N]

WHITE MAN RACIST NOMINEE WOULD BE FORCED TO WITHDRAW. LATINA WOMAN RACIST SHOULD ALSO WITHDRAW.

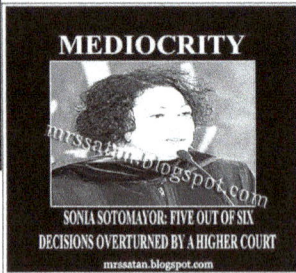

THERE WERE UGLY, DEMEANING IMAGES OF HER CIRCULATED ON THE INTERNET.

FOR HER PART, SONIA KEPT HER HEAD UP, AND SIMPLY WENT ABOUT THE BUSINESS OF MEETING THE SENATORS WHO WOULD VOTE ON HER NOMINATION, TO SHARE WITH THEM HER JUDICIAL PHILOSOPHY.

DEFEAT SOTOMAYOR

MEDIOCRITY

mrssatan.blogspot.com

SONIA SOTOMAYOR: FIVE OUT OF SIX DECISIONS OVERTURNED BY A HIGHER COURT
mrssatan.blogspot.com

Sexism, Racism, Activism In Sonya Sotomayor's Court nothing is what it seems

THE CRYING GAME
...confirm her at your own risk

WHITES GET OUT!
Aztlan
THIS IS ARE LAND
LA RAZA
HOPE CHANGE

We the People

WHICH WAS KIND OF HARD TO DO, CONSIDERING SHE HAD RECENTLY BROKEN HER ANKLE WHILE RUNNING TO CATCH A PLANE AT THE AIRPORT.

WHEN THE SENATE JUDICIARY COMMITTEE HEARING ON HER NOMINATION CAME TO ORDER ON JULY 13TH, SONIA WAS BACK ON HER FEET—AND FIGHTING BACK AGAINST CHARGES THAT SHE PUT HER SYMPATHY FOR CERTAIN ETHNIC GROUPS ABOVE THE LAW.

I DO NOT BELIEVE THAT ANY ETHNIC, RACIAL OR GENDER GROUP HAS AN ADVANTAGE IN SOUND JUDGMENT.

SHE FACED TOUGH QUESTIONS FROM REPUBLICANS ABOUT HER REPUTATION FOR ASKING TOUGH QUESTIONS OF THE LAWYERS WHO ARGUED BEFORE HER.

DO YOU THINK YOU HAVE A TEMPERAMENT PROBLEM?

IN THE END, SHE PREVAILED BY A 13-6 VOTE OF THE JUDICIARY COMMITTEE. THE FULL SENATE WOULD VOTE TO CONFIRM HER ON AUGUST 6, 2009

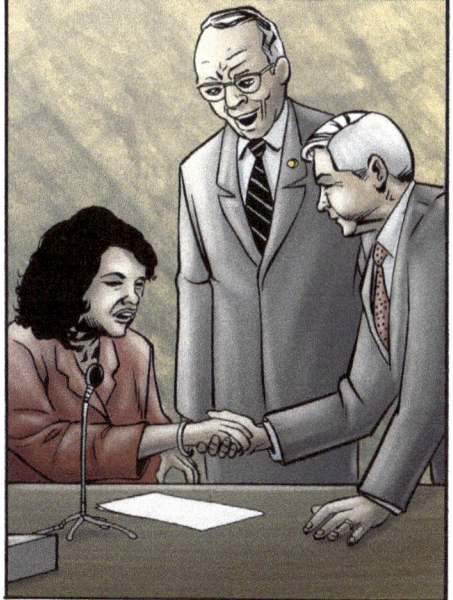

ALL THAT LAY AHEAD NOW WAS THE ARRIVAL OF FALL—AND A CHANCE FOR JUDGE SOTOMAYOR TO TAKE HER RIGHTFUL PLACE ON AMERICA'S HIGHEST COURT.

I KNOW ONE THING...YOU CAN BET YOUR BOTTOM DOLLAR THOSE SUPREME COURT GET-TOGETHERS ARE GOING TO BE A WHOLE LOT MORE INTERESTING FROM NOW ON!

WELCOME, JUSTICE SOTOMAYOR!

KISS THE COOK

BLUEWATER COMICS

★ FEMALE ★ FORCE ★

Sonia Sotomayor

Robert Schnakenberg — Writer

Cesar Feliciano — Penciler

Kirsty Swan — Colorist

Wilson Ramos Jr. — Letterer

Darren G. Davis — Graphics

Darren G. Davis
Publisher

Jason Schultz
Vice President

Lisa K. Brause
Entertainment Manager

Crystal VanDiver
Director

Lisa Battan
Marketing Director

Janda Tithia
Coordinator

Scott Davis
Media Manager

Kim Sherman
Marketing Director

Vonnie Harris
New Business

Adam Ellis
Coordinator

Cover: Joshua LaBello & Azim

Patrick Foster
Logo Design

Adam Ellis
Production

BLUEWATER COMICS

www.bluewaterprod.com

#ERASEHATE WITH THE
MATTHEW SHEPARD FOUNDATION

With your donated dollars and volunteer hours, we work tirelessly to erase hate from every corner of America through our programs.

SPEAKING ENGAGEMENTS

Since Matt's death in 1998, Judy and Dennis have been determined to prevent others from similar tragedies. By sharing their story, they are able to carry on Matt's legacy.

HATE CRIMES REPORTING

Our work to improve reporting includes conducting trainings for law enforcement agencies, building relationships between community leaders and law enforcement, and developing policy reform in reporting practices.

LARAMIE PROJECT

MSF offers support to productions of The Laramie Project, which depicts the events leading up to and after Matt's murder. It remains one of the most performed plays in America.

MATTHEW'S PLACE

MatthewsPlace.com is a blog designed to provide young LGBTQ+ people with an outlet for their voices. From finance to health to love and dating, and everything in between, our writers contribute excellent material.

Erase Hate

Matthew
Shepard
Foundation
embracing diversity

WHEN THE SENATE JUDICIARY COMMITTEE HEARING ON HER NOMINATION CAME TO ORDER ON JULY 13TH, SONIA WAS BACK ON HER FEET—AND FIGHTING BACK AGAINST CHARGES THAT SHE PUT HER SYMPATHY FOR CERTAIN ETHNIC GROUPS ABOVE THE LAW.

I DO NOT BELIEVE THAT ANY ETHNIC, RACIAL OR GENDER GROUP HAS AN ADVANTAGE IN SOUND JUDGMENT.

SHE FACED TOUGH QUESTIONS FROM REPUBLICANS ABOUT HER REPUTATION FOR ASKING TOUGH QUESTIONS OF THE LAWYERS WHO ARGUED BEFORE HER.

DO YOU THINK YOU HAVE A TEMPERAMENT PROBLEM?

IN THE END, SHE PREVAILED BY A 13-6 VOTE OF THE JUDICIARY COMMITTEE. THE FULL SENATE WOULD VOTE TO CONFIRM HER ON AUGUST 6, 2009

ALL THAT LAY AHEAD NOW WAS THE ARRIVAL OF FALL—AND A CHANCE FOR JUDGE SOTOMAYOR TO TAKE HER RIGHTFUL PLACE ON AMERICA'S HIGHEST COURT.

I KNOW ONE THING...YOU CAN BET YOUR BOTTOM DOLLAR THOSE SUPREME COURT GET-TOGETHERS ARE GOING TO BE A WHOLE LOT MORE INTERESTING FROM NOW ON!

WELCOME, JUSTICE SOTOMAYOR!

KISS THE COOK

www.ingramcontent.com/pod-product-compliance
Lightning Source LLC
Chambersburg PA
CBHW081236020426
42331CB00012B/3196